Flowchart Smart

THE SCIENCE OF WETLANDS

I0809339

Richard and Louise Spilsbury

Gareth Stevens PUBLISHING

Please visit our website, **www.garethstevens.com**.
For a free color catalog of all our high-quality books,
call toll free 1-800-542-2595 or fax 1-877-542-2596.

Cataloging-in-Publication Data

Names: Spilsbury, Richard. | Spilsbury, Louise.
Title: Wetlands / Richard and Louise Spilsbury.
Description: New York : Gareth Stevens Publishing, 2020. | Series: Flowchart smart | Includes glossary and index.
Identifiers: ISBN 9781538252345 (pbk.) | ISBN 9781538252352 (library bound)
Subjects: LCSH: Wetlands--Juvenile literature.
Classification: LCC QH87.3 S65 2020 | DDC 333.91'8--dc23

First Edition

Published in 2020 by
Gareth Stevens Publishing
111 East 14th Street, Suite 349
New York, NY 10003

© 2020 Gareth Stevens Publishing

Produced for Gareth Stevens by Calcium
Editors: Sarah Eason and Harriet McGregor
Designer: Emma DeBanks
Picture researcher: Rachel Blount

Picture credits: Cover: Shutterstock: Azuzi (c), Tayka Ya (br); Inside: Shutterstock: Hiromi Ito Ame: pp. 44-45; Azuzl: p. 17; Billedfab: p. 43; Steve Bower: pp. 10-11; Buteo: p. 5t; Steve Byland: p. 22b; Jayne Chapman: p. 10b; Chevonski: pp. 26-27; Clarst5: pp. 28-29; CrackerClips Stock Media: pp. 36-37; Eye-blink: pp. 14-15; Feel4nature: p 26; Arto Hakola: p. 35b; I Wei Huang: pp. 40-41; Sarin Kunthong: pp. 1, 21t; Linas T: pp 12-13; Lukaszsokol: p. 29t; Macrovector: pp. 24-25; Alun Marchant: p. 7t; Leonardo Mercon: pp. 4-5; Kylie Nicholson: pp. 18-19, 31t; NomadFra: pp. 6-7; Oxie99: p. 15t; Roop_Dey: p. 41t; SaveJungle: pp. 32-33, 39; Petr Simon: p. 19b; Stihii: p. 8; Decha Thapanya: p. 13r; Sergey Uryadnikov: pp. 22-23; Jeffry Weymier: p. 37t; aDam Wildlife: pp. 20-21; Vladimir Wrangel: pp. 30-31; Yhelfman: pp. 34-35; I. Noyan Yilmaz: p. 45r.

All rights reserved. No part of this book may be reproduced in any form
without permission from the publisher, except by a reviewer.

Printed in the United States of America

CPSIA compliance information: Batch #CW20GS: For further information contact Gareth Stevens, New York, New York at 1-800-542-2595.

Contents

Chapter 1

What Are Wetlands?

A wetland is an area of **waterlogged** land where water covers or soaks into the soil for long periods of the year. Wetlands are amazing **ecosystems** that are home to fish and other wildlife.

Wetlands are often found alongside waterways, such as streams and rivers, and in areas of low-lying ground. Many wetlands are wet all year round. Others are covered in water for part of the year because water levels change with the seasons. Some wetlands are wetter during annual rains. Some are covered alternately with freshwater and salty seawater. One of the things that makes wetlands special is their **saturated** soils. These soils have less **oxygen** in them than other soils. That is why only certain plants and animals are adapted to live there.

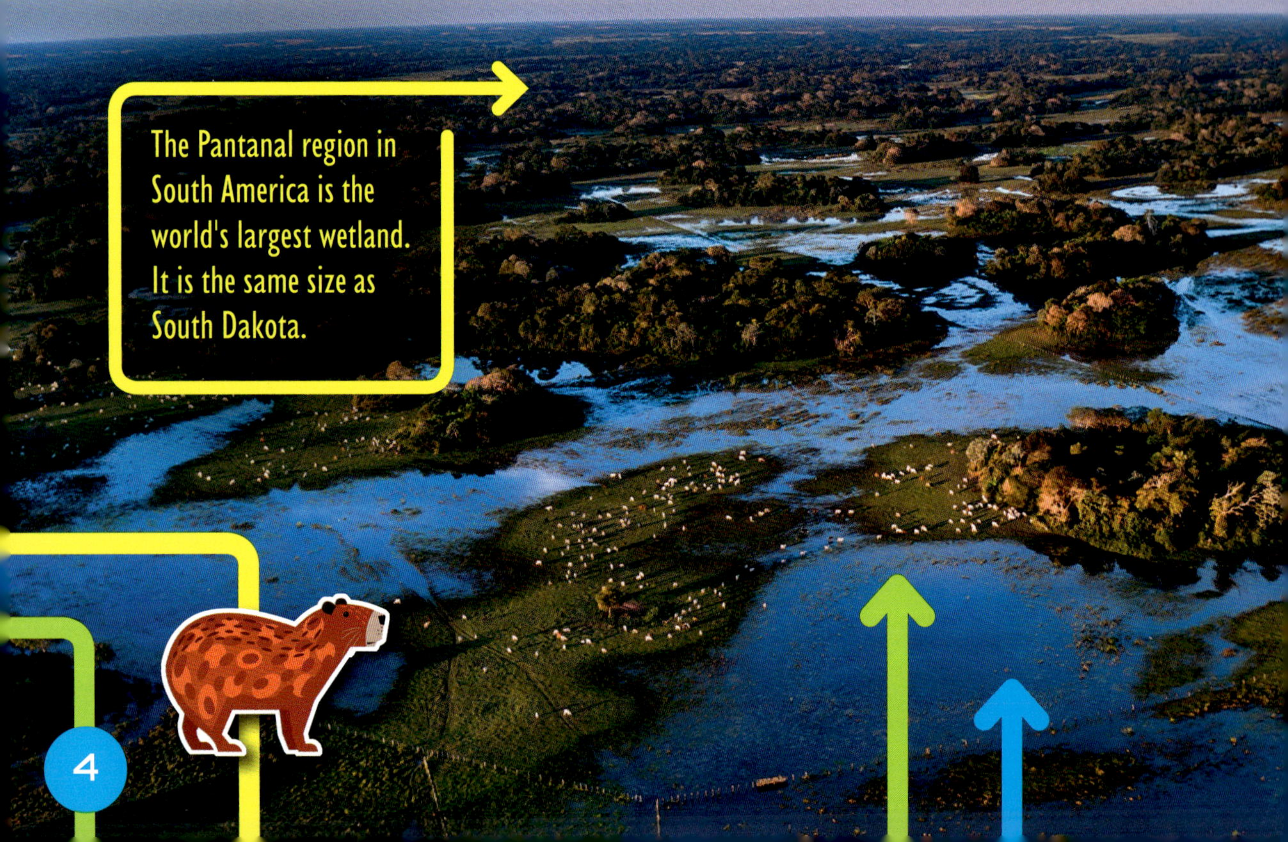

The Pantanal region in South America is the world's largest wetland. It is the same size as South Dakota.

An ecosystem is made up of all the living and nonliving things that **interact** with each other in an area. Living things include plants and animals and nonliving things include the weather, sunlight, water, and soil. All ecosystems have their own unique and special features. The wetland ecosystem includes everything in the wetland, from the water and the wet, muddy soils to a wide range of animals from tiny fish to huge hippos.

Capybaras live in the Pantanal. They feed on water plants and use water to hide from danger.

Get Smart!

There are wetlands in many different types of **climates**, from cold and wet to hot and steamy. There are wetlands on every continent except Antarctica. Wetlands vary in size from single potholes on the Great Plains of the United States, which fill with water in the spring, to the Pantanal in Brazil, Bolivia, and Paraguay, which covers 75,000 square miles (195,000 square km). During the rainy season in the Pantanal, the water levels can rise by almost 16 ft (5 m).

Types of Wetland

There are different types of wetlands and there are many different names for them, including swamps, bogs, fens, marshes, mangroves, mudflats, and deltas. Most wetlands can be divided into two groups: inland and coastal.

Inland wetlands are most common near rivers and streams, in depressions in the ground that fill with water after heavy rains. Inland wetlands are also found along the edges of lakes and ponds, and in other low-lying areas where the water seeps up from underground **aquifers** or springs. Inland wetlands include marshes, wet meadows, and swamps that form where a lake has gradually filled with mud and plants.

Get Smart!

Deltas form where rivers meet an ocean or lake. Streams and rivers begin in hills and mountains. They flow quickly over high ground, and as they do so, they pick up sediment from the land, such as mud, rock, and sand. As the river approaches the ocean, the land becomes flatter. Rivers widen and the water flow slows down. Here, the river drops its sediment. Some of it washes into the ocean and some of it settles and forms a flat, muddy area. This is the delta.

This is a coastal swamp. It is filled with grass and other plants. The swamp is connected by a shallow sea to the ocean.

The plains of the Okavango Delta in Botswana, Africa, flood seasonally. They are an inland wetland.

Coastal wetlands are sometimes called tidal wetlands because they are found where rivers meet the sea. These wetland ecosystems can be covered with fresh river water for part of the day, and then become covered with salty seawater when the tide comes in. These twice-daily changes create a challenging ecosystem for plants and animals. They must be able to cope with both salt water and freshwater. They must also cope with being exposed to the air for some of the time, too. Saltwater swamps like this are usually found along **tropical** coastlines.

Get flowchart smart!

How Deltas Form

Let's follow the steps in the formation of a delta wetland.

Deltas form as rivers gradually deposit sediment into another body of water, such as a sea, ocean, or lake.

The sea may carry this sediment away, or it may settle to form a flat, muddy area called a delta.

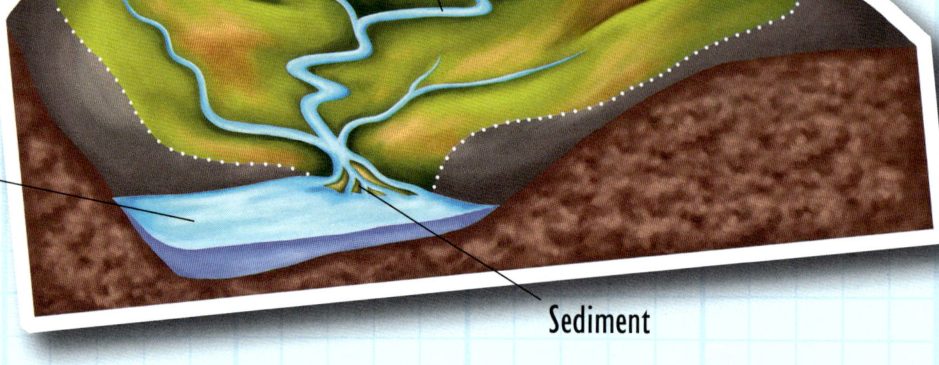

Rivers usually begin on high ground, where they flow quickly.

When rivers flow into the ocean, they are moving slowly over flatter land.

As they move more slowly, rivers drop their sediment. This is their load of mud, rock, and sand washed from higher ground.

Flowchart Smart

Chapter 2

Wetland Plants

There is a huge variety of wetland plants, ranging from tiny plants that float at the water's surface to giant trees that have their roots in muddy wetland soils.

Grasses such as cattails, bulrush, and sedges are common in wetlands. They can grow with their lower parts underwater and their upper parts above it. They have an extensive network of roots to anchor themselves in the soggy wetland soils. Some sedges produce underground stems called rhizomes, which spread rapidly through the mud. This allows new plants to emerge away from the parent plant to grow in new areas of mud. Bulrushes have tall stems that allow their roots to anchor in the mud while they hold their feathery flower heads high above the water. They produce large seed heads that provide a valuable food source and nesting material for water birds.

Cypress swamps are the most famous type of swamplands in the United States. Swamp cypress trees are large conifer trees that have roots that grow and spread widely around the base of the trees to support them. The roots trap sediment from the water, creating a kind of private island that supports the tree in the soft, shifting mud below it. Spanish moss grows on the tree branches for support and traps water from rain, fog, and water vapor in the air in tiny hairlike parts called trichomes.

The trees in this swamp are surrounded by duckweed plants that float on the surface of the wetland water.

Swamp cypress trees grow slowly and live a very long time. Their wide buttress roots firmly anchor them in the swamp.

Get Smart!

Duckweed often forms a green carpet on the surface of a freshwater wetland. Duckweed plants have tiny, hairlike roots that dangle in the water below the plant. The roots absorb the water and **nutrients** the plants need to survive. Duckweed plants have two tiny leaflike parts that are fleshy and filled with air. These keep the plant afloat on the surface of the water.

Carnivorous Plants

Waste decays, or breaks down, very slowly in wet soils. This means that wetland soils do not release nutrients that help other living things grow. In swamps and bogs, **carnivorous** plants catch insects to supplement their diet.

Venus flytraps are carnivorous plants. Nectar in their leaves attracts their victims.

The Venus flytrap has leaves that are adapted to open and close and catch insects. When an insect lands on a leaf and touches one of the tiny trigger hairs on it, the leaves snap together quickly—in less than a second. The leaves are edged with spikes that form a cage to keep the trapped insect from escaping. Over around a week, digestive juices **dissolve** the insect, and the Venus flytrap plant absorbs this nutrient-rich "soup" as food. After this, the plant is ready for another meal, so the trap opens again.

Pitcher plants grow in marshes. These plants are adapted to have strange, pitcher-shaped leaves that contain digestive juices. The pitcher releases a smell that attracts insects. When an insect lands on the leaf, it slides down its slippery sides into the digestive juices. There, the juices slowly digest the insect so the plant can use the nutrients from it inside its body.

Get Smart!

Some underwater wetland plants catch animals, too. Bladderworts are the fastest carnivorous plants on the planet. Bladderworts have small, hollow sacs that trap, capture, and digest tiny animals such as insect larvae, worms, and water fleas. When the **prey** animal accidentally touches trigger hairs on the surface of the trap door, it suddenly opens, sucks in the prey, and closes again in just a fraction of a second.

Most pitcher plants contain downward-pointing hairs inside the pitcher to keep prey from climbing out.

Coastal Wetland Plants

Most plants are unable to survive in wetlands. This is because there is not enough oxygen in the soil for them and salt water dries them out. Some plants are specially adapted to cope with these challenges.

Mangrove trees thrive on muddy tropical shores where the soils are low in oxygen and the slow-moving water leaves thick mud deposits. Most mangrove roots grow out from halfway up the tree trunk, then grow downward into the mud. Part of these roots remain above water even when the tide is in, taking in oxygen through special pores, or holes, and supplying it to the waterlogged roots. The root parts in the mud anchor the mangrove tree as waves move in and out and the mud shifts below.

A mangrove forest is made up of many trees. Their roots act like stilts to hold the top of the tree above the water.

Get Smart!

Mangrove trees are an important part of their wetland ecosystem. Their tangled roots help to stabilize the coastline, keeping waves from washing away the muddy soils. The root systems also provide shelter and food for many fish and other wetland animals.

In salt marshes or **estuaries**, many plants take in freshwater when they can and store it in fleshy stems and leaves for later, when the tide comes in. The glasswort plant stores water in bright green, fleshy stems. Other plants have leaves with leathery surfaces, which prevent water from moving out of the plant and into the salt water. Salt marsh cordgrass is adapted to take up salt water through its roots. It then gets rid of the salt through tiny pores called stomata on the underside of its leaves.

Glasswort plants store water so they can survive on beaches and on salt marshes.

How a Venus Flytrap Works

Let's discover how a Venus flytrap works.

The Venus flytrap has leaves adapted to open and shut like a trap.

Over around a week, digestive juices dissolve the insect and the Venus flytrap plant absorbs this nutrient-rich "soup" as food.

Then, the plant is ready for another meal, so the trap opens again.

When an insect lands on a leaf and touches one of the tiny trigger hairs on it, the leaves snap together quickly—in less than a second.

The leaves are edged with spikes that form a cage to keep the trapped insects from escaping.

Flowchart Smart

Chapter 3

Animal Adaptations

Adaptations are special behaviors, features, or body parts that living things develop over time to help them survive in an ecosystem. In wetlands, animals must adapt to survive both in water and on land.

The capybara is the world's biggest **rodent** and is adapted for life in the wetlands of Central and South America. Its **webbed** feet help it walk on land and swim in water. A layer of fat beneath its skin helps it float in the water. Its eyes, ears, and nostrils are all near the top of its head so it can rest underwater but can still see, hear, and smell what is going on nearby. Its long, sharp front teeth are adapted to bite off tough water plants to eat.

Capybaras keep cool in shallow water and mud during the day. They graze during the evening.

Get Smart!

Beavers are a type of rodent that has huge teeth. A beaver uses its teeth to strip bark and leaves from trees for food. It gnaws logs off small trees and uses them to make a den in a wetland. Beavers raise young in the den and hide there to escape from **predators**.

The shoebill is a very large wetland bird. It has a huge bill, or beak, which looks like the front end of a boot. It is very thick and heavy and has a sharp hook at the end. The shoebill stands in wetlands on its long legs and waits for a fish, frog, turtle, or snake to pass by. Then it quickly shoots its head forward at the same time as it opens its bill. The sharp edges of the bill can grab, crush, and pierce the body of its often slippery prey before the bird swallows it down.

The shoebill lives in wetlands across Africa. Large fish such as lungfish are its favorite food.

On the Move

The mud that covers the wetland floor can be sticky and difficult to move across. Some animals have interesting adaptations to help them cope with these challenges.

Mudskippers are a type of wetland fish. They can survive out of water for up to two and a half hours.

A mudskipper can swim in wetland water but also crawl on mud. In water, it swims like a fish, often with its head above the water, but it can also flip its tail from side to side and skip across the surface of the water. Out of water, a mudskipper uses its adapted fins a little like legs to walk, jump, and climb. It holds its body straight and flips forward on its fins in little skipping movements. It leaves the water to find food and also to move between wetland pools.

Adult dragonflies avoid mud and water by flying above the wetland. They have four wings, which they use to fly directly upward and downward or to hover in one spot. They speed across wetland water, looking for insects, such as mosquitoes, to eat. Dragonflies have enormous eyes that take up most of the space on their head. These help them locate tiny prey in any direction, which they swoop down and snatch up in their feet!

Dragonflies catch up to 95 percent of the insect prey they chase after.

Get Smart!

While mudskippers are in water, they breathe through parts called **gills** like regular fish. When they are on land, these highly unusual fish absorb oxygen directly from the air. They take in the oxygen through their skin and through the lining of their mouth. That is why they are often seen with their mouths open, gulping for air.

Life Cycles

Many birds, insects, and other animals are adapted to complete important stages in their **life cycles** in wetlands.

Damselflies and dragonflies lay eggs in wetland water. The larvae, or young, that hatch out of the eggs spend the first one or two years of their lives in water. When they are fully grown, the larvae crawl up a plant stem and out of the water. Their outer skin breaks open and sheds to reveal the insect's wings. The insects wait a few hours for their wings to dry out and harden. Then they can begin to fly above the wetland water, catching small, flying insect prey to eat.

Frogs also start their lives in wetland water. When they first hatch from eggs, they are tadpoles. Tadpoles have a long tail that they wave from side to side for swimming. As the tadpoles grow and turn into frogs, they get bigger and bigger. Legs form and gradually the tail is absorbed into their body. After the tadpoles have become frogs, they mainly live on land. They return to water when it is time for them to lay eggs, and another wetland life cycle begins.

This young frog has grown legs but it still has its tadpole tail.

Flamingos nests are made of mud, stones, straw, and feathers. They can be up to 12 inches (30 cm) high.

Get Smart!

Flamingos have a behavioral adaptation for wetland breeding. Parent birds use their bills to scrape mud into high mounds. They lay an egg in a dip at the top, so it cannot roll off. This protects the egg from wetland floods, which could wash it away.

Get flowchart smart!

A Frog Life Cycle

Discover the secret of a wetland frog's life cycle.

Frogs begin their lives as eggs in wetland water.

After the tadpoles have become frogs, they mainly live on land. They return to water when it is time for them to lay eggs. Then, another wetland life cycle begins.

When they first hatch from their eggs, they are tadpoles.

Tadpoles have a long tail. To swim, they wave it from side to side.

As the tadpoles gradually turn into frogs, they grow bigger and bigger and begin to grow legs.

The tail is gradually absorbed into the body.

Flowchart Smart

Chapter 4
Food Chains

All living things in an ecosystem need food to give them energy to grow, move, hunt, and survive. The lives of all the living things in a wetland are linked together in thousands of different food chains, which all begin with plants.

Wetland plants are first in the food chain because they produce their own food. Plants take **carbon dioxide** from the air into their leaves. They take water in through their roots. A green substance called chlorophyll in the leaves traps energy from sunlight. This energy is used to turn carbon dioxide and water into sugar that is used and stored in the plant for food. This process is called **photosynthesis**. Carnivorous wetland plants also get some nutrients from insects and other animals they digest.

Manatees live in tropical wetlands. They have short front flippers and a flat tail, which they use to swim. They also use their flippers to crawl.

The second link in food chains are **herbivores**. Many herbivores, such as crabs and shellfish, live among mangrove roots and feed on fallen leaves and other material. Large animals eat wetland plants, too. In wetlands in the Congo, in Africa, buffalo, elephants, and gorillas visit wetlands to eat the plants there. Manatees are large, gray mammals that live in warm and shallow coastal wetlands around the Caribbean Sea, the Gulf of Mexico, the southern Atlantic coast of the United States, and northern South America. They feed on beds of seagrass in the water. They have a strong, flexible upper lip that can grasp and rip out whole plants.

Get Smart!

Muskrats are commonly found in the wetlands of North America. This rodent has four chisel-like front teeth that protrude ahead of the cheeks, and lips that close behind them. This allows the muskrat to gnaw on roots and stems underwater with its mouth closed!

Mangrove crabs use their claws to grab food and put it into their mouth. They burrow in the ground or climb trees to escape predators.

Secondary Consumers

Many wetland animals are secondary **consumers**: they feed on herbivores or carnivores. Smaller secondary consumers are themselves eaten by larger secondary consumers.

Many wetland insects feed on other insects or insect larvae. Water striders are insects that live on the water's surface. They use their middle legs as paddles to move across the water. Their back legs help them steer to chase prey. Their short front legs are used to grab small insects to eat, which they do by sucking out the body juices of their victims. Great diving beetles are large beetles that can store bubbles of air beneath their wings, like a scuba tank. They dive underwater to hunt small animals, such as other insects, tadpoles, snails, and even small fish, all the time breathing from the air bubble.

The great diving beetle is an aggressive predator that catches and eats a wide variety of prey in its wetland home.

Many birds feed on wetland insects and fish. Great egrets stand and feed in shallow water. They wait patiently for fish, frogs, or insects to pass by, and then spear their food using their long, sharp bills. Black egrets, a type of African heron, spread their wings as they walk slowly through the shallow waters of a wetland. Fish prey are attracted to the shade. Once in the shade, it is also easier for the heron to spot them.

The bar-tailed godwit is a long-billed, long-legged wading bird that feeds on mollusks, worms, and insects.

Get Smart!

Many **migratory** birds, such as whooping cranes and peregrine falcons, stop over at wetlands to rest and eat during their long migrations. The bar-tailed godwit migrates from Alaska to New Zealand each September and back again each March. It could not survive the journey without feeding at wetlands along the way.

Perfect Predators

At the top of wetland food chains are the apex, or top, predators. These are the hunters that catch and kill other animals, but are too big or dangerous to have any natural predators themselves.

Anacondas are the largest snakes in the world. They swim well and kill prey such as caimans by coiling their muscular bodies around the prey and strangling them. If that does not work, they drown them. Caimans hide underwater with their eyes, nose, and ears above the surface so they can still detect prey. When an animal visits the water to drink, the caimans strike. They lunge forward to grab large animals, such as capybara or wild boar, in their sharp teeth. Caimans have many teeth. If one falls out during an attack on their prey, a new one simply replaces it.

Anacondas have jaws that can open so wide they can swallow their prey whole, no matter how big it is.

Harpy eagles fly from rain forest trees over nearby wetlands in search of prey. They can swoop down and catch ocelots, a type of wild cat, in their talons. Ocelots can be found hunting alone at night in mangrove forests and marshes, where they climb, jump, and even swim in their efforts to find food. Ocelots track their prey by scent and eat small rodents, which in turn eat plants in the wetlands.

This caiman has caught a piranha, a fish known for its razor-sharp teeth and dangerous bite.

Get Smart!

A large caiman can sometimes win a battle with an anaconda, and eat the snake instead of being eaten itself! While adult apex predators are safe, their young are not so safe. For example, many baby anaconda and caiman are eaten by a variety of wetland predators.

Get flowchart smart!

A Wetland Food Chain

Let's take a look at a wetland food chain.

Wetland plants use the process of photosynthesis to make their own food, some of which they store in body parts such as stems and leaves.

Anacondas are snakes that swim well and kill prey, such as caimans, by coiling their muscular bodies around the prey and strangling them. Anacondas are apex predators.

Capybaras are large rodents that use their sharp teeth to feed on parts of wetland plants.

Caimans hide underwater with their eyes, nose and ears above the surface so they can still detect prey. When an animal visits the water to drink, the caimans strike. They lunge forward to grab their prey in their sharp teeth.

Chapter 5

Wetland Interactions

The different living and nonliving parts of a wetland ecosystem rely on one another to survive. The special way the different parts of the ecosystem interact keeps it healthy.

Wetland plants hold wetland soil together. Their roots bind the soil and keep it from being washed away by heavy rains or flooding. This is particularly important in coastal regions, because anchoring soils and sand in this way can prevent the coastal wetlands from being destroyed altogether. Wetland plants also slow the flow of water, which helps the wetland ecosystem to store water. This is important because storing water is what defines a wetland, and it prevents wetlands from drying out completely during drier seasons.

The grasses of the Alviso wetlands in California give protection to young fish.

Get Smart!

Wetland plants, such as seagrasses, also play an important role in the ecosystem because they provide shelter for young fish. The fish live among the grasses until they are better able to swim fast enough to evade predators. This keeps fish populations in the wetland ecosystem healthy.

Living things that break down plant and animal remains and waste also keep wetland soils healthy. **Scavengers** are animals that eat rotting plants and the remains of dead animals. Crayfish are scavengers. They help keep wetlands clean and break up remains so that **decomposers** can get to work on them. Decomposers such as **bacteria** break down the remains into nutrients. They feed on some of these nutrients and the rest wash into the wetland soil. The nutrients help more plants grow. By **recycling** nutrients in this way, decomposers start new food chains.

The turkey vulture is a scavenger that lives in the wetlands in Florida. It uses its eyesight and sense of smell to locate dead animals.

Helping Out

Some animals help their wetland ecosystems in important ways. Birds rest at wetlands when they migrate long distances from their breeding areas to their wintering areas. In doing so, they spread wetland plants. Birds such as mallard ducks, for example, feed largely on plant seeds. Many of the seeds that they eat have tough seed covers and they are not fully digested. Instead, the seeds survive intact until they are passed out in the mallard's feces. In this way, the mallards play an important role in carrying the seeds and spreading wetland plants in new areas. This ensures that there is a diverse range of plants in the wetlands, which encourages other wildlife, too.

Some animals are so important to their ecosystem that they are known as keystone species. In the coastal wetlands of Louisiana, American alligators are a keystone species. They are powerful predators that eat large numbers of gar and other predatory fish, which prevents those fish from eating too many other fish. When they use their claws and jaws to dig holes, water collects in the holes. This helps other animals in the dry season. Their hole-digging also creates a boggy type of soil that helps plants grow. The mounds that alligators make for their nests are used by other animals as nests or as places to escape floods after the alligator babies have hatched from their eggs and left.

American alligators live in swamps in several states in the southeastern United States.

Mallards live in northern wetland nesting grounds in the summer, and southern wetland resting grounds in the winter.

Get Smart!

Alligators wait below bird nests so they can eat young fledgling birds that fall as they leave the nest. In turn, the alligators help the adult birds because the alligators eat raccoons, which prey on the birds, fledglings, and the eggs.

Get flowchart smart!

Why Alligators Are a Keystone Species

Let's discover what makes American alligators a keystone species.

In the coastal wetlands of Louisiana, American alligators are a keystone species.

American alligators build mounds for their nests. These are used by other animals as nests or as places to escape floods after the alligator babies have hatched from their eggs and left.

American alligators help birds by eating raccoons that would otherwise eat the birds and their offspring.

American alligators are powerful predators. They eat large numbers of gar and other predatory fish, which prevents these fish from eating too many other fish.

They use their claws and jaws to dig holes. Water collects in the holes, which helps other animals in the drier seasons.

Their hole-digging also helps create a boggy type of soil in which plants grow well.

Flowchart Smart

Chapter 6

The Future for Wetland Ecosystems

Human activities and changes to wetlands risk putting entire ecosystems out of balance and under threat.

Sometimes, wetlands are drained so the land they occupy can be built on.

The world's wetlands are under threat for different reasons. In some areas, people drain, or remove the water, from wetlands so that they can build homes or offices, or to create farmland. Wetlands may also lose their water if the water is diverted via channels into fields to water crops. Other wetlands are polluted when chemicals from factories, power plants, or sewage farms wash into them.

The biggest threat facing wetlands is **climate change**. As parts of the world get hotter, the amount of rain that falls there is lessening, which increases the risk of drought. Given that water is already in short supply in some wetlands at certain times of the year, the reduced rainfall increases the risk that some wetlands will dry up completely. Climate change is also melting polar ice and causing sea levels to rise. As sea levels rise, they could totally submerge and destroy some coastal wetlands.

Wetlands such as the Sundarbans, in Bangladesh, where this Bengal tiger lives, are at risk from sea level rise.

Get Smart!

Water pollution damages wetlands. Chemicals found in sewage and cleaning products encourage **algae** to grow in the water. The algae spreads and forms large, slimy mats that cover the water and block sunlight. Other plants die because they do not have enough light. When the algae die, the bacteria that decomposes them use up a lot of oxygen. This reduces the amount of available oxygen in the water for other living things to use.

Get flowchart smart!

How Pollution Damages Wetlands

Follow the steps in the process by which pollution can damage a wetland ecosystem.

Water pollution causes serious problems for wetlands.

When algae die, the bacteria that decompose them use up a lot of oxygen. This reduces the amount of oxygen left in the water for other living things to use.

With less light and oxygen, fewer plants can grow. With fewer plants to feed on, there are fewer animals.

Chemicals called nitrates found in sewage, for example, encourage algae to grow in the water.

The algae spreads and forms large, slimy mats that cover the water and block the sunlight that living things in the water need.

Protecting Wetland Ecosystems

Wetlands are among the rarest and the most threatened ecosystems in the world. Many people are working hard to protect wetlands.

Governments make laws to keep people from taking over wetlands. In many places, it is against the law to dump waste, cut down plants and trees, or pour dirt into a wetland. **Conservation** groups raise money to help protect endangered wetlands and wildlife. In some places, governments and conservation groups help pay for wetland **reserves**. These are wetlands that are completely protected by law and that no one is allowed to alter or damage in any way.

We can all help wetlands by doing what we can to slow down climate change. Reducing energy use can slow down climate change. Reduce your fuel and electricity use, for example, by cycling instead of traveling by car and by putting on a sweater instead of turning the heat up. Ask your family to choose refrigerators and other appliances that use less energy. Change to energy-efficient light bulbs and unplug computers, televisions, and other electronic devices when not in use. Wetlands are an amazing ecosystem, and we should all do all we can to help them have a healthy future.

At the moment, around 40 percent of Africa's Okavango Delta is within a wildlife reserve and is protected by law. Scientists and other groups also want to protect the waterways that feed the Okavango Delta.

People who manage wetland reserves keep them safe from damage and help keep them healthy, for example, by organizing litter cleanups and checking for water pollution levels.

Get Smart!

Wetlands are important ecosystems, and they help us, too. Wetlands act like giant sponges, soaking up water and keeping it from flooding areas of dry land where people live. Wetland plants also help filter the water and make it clean.

Glossary

adaptations Changes to suit a new situation.

algae Plantlike living things found in damp places.

aquifers Areas of rock beneath Earth's surface that absorb and hold water.

bacteria Tiny living things that can help decompose waste.

carbon dioxide A gas in the air.

carnivorous Meat-eating.

climates The general weather that happens in regions over many years.

climate change A change in the pattern of the world's weather caused by Earth's atmosphere getting warmer.

conservation The act of guarding, protecting, or preserving something.

consumers Animals that eat plants or other animals.

decomposers Living things that break down waste.

dissolve Broken down and absorbed by a liquid.

ecosystems The living and nonliving things in a place, interacting with one another.

estuaries Places where a river meets an ocean.

gills Body parts that fish and some other animals use to breathe underwater.

herbivores Animals that eat only plants.

interact Act in such a way as to have an effect on one another.

life cycles The series of changes in the life of a living thing.

migratory Traveling long distances when the season changes.

nutrients Substances that living things need to survive and grow.

oxygen A gas found in air and water that animals need to survive.

photosynthesis The process by which green plants make sugary food using the energy in sunlight.

predators Animals that catch and eat other animals.

prey An animal hunted and eaten by another animal.

recycling Converting to something new.

reserves Protected areas that keep living things and landscapes of special interest safe from destruction.

rodent A small animal with large, sharp front teeth, such as a mouse or rat.

saturated Holding as much water or moisture as can be absorbed.

scavengers Animals that feed on dead animals, plants, or waste.

tropical Found in places near the equator, which are warm all year round.

waterlogged Full of water.

webbed Having skin between the toes or fingers.

For More Information

Books

Barghoorn, Linda. *Map and Track Wetlands* (Map and Track Biomes and Animals). New York, NY: Crabtree Publishing Company, 2019.

O'Sullivan, J.K. *Marshes and Swamps!: With 25 Science Projects for Kids* (Explore Your World). White River Junction, VT: Nomad Press, 2018.

Perdew, Laura. *Bringing Back Our Wetlands* (Conservation Success Stories). North Mankato, MN: Essential Library, 2018.

Sidabras, Kimberly. *Wetlands* (World's Biomes). Broomall, PA: Mason Crest Publishers, 2018.

Websites

Discover more about the United States' wetlands at:
www.epa.gov/wetlands

Visit the National Geographic website for more information about and photographs of wetlands:
www.nationalgeographic.org/encyclopedia/wetland

Find out more about bogs, swamps, marshes, and other wetlands at:
www.nps.gov/piro/learn/nature/wetlands.htm

Watch this movie for an explanation of wetlands at:
oceanservice.noaa.gov/facts/wetland.html

Publisher's note to educators and parents: Our editors have carefully reviewed these websites to ensure that they are suitable for students. Many websites change frequently, however, and we cannot guarantee that a site's future contents will continue to meet our high standards of quality and educational value. Be advised that students should be closely supervised whenever they access the Internet.

Index